'SHE WA_ _ AND FO___ _ AGAINST HER BOREDOM, WHICH ONLY BORED HER STILL MORE.'

JAVIER MARÍAS
Born 1951, Madrid, Spain

All essays are taken from *Written Lives*, first published in Spain
as *Vidas Escritas* in 2000.

JAVIER MARÍAS

Madame du Deffand and the Idiots

Translated by Margaret Jull Costa

PENGUIN BOOKS

PENGUIN CLASSICS

UK | USA | Canada | Ireland | Australia
India | New Zealand | South Africa

Penguin Books is part of the Penguin Random House group
of companies whose addresses can be found at
global.penguinrandomhouse.com.

Penguin
Random House
UK

This selection first published 2018

001

Set in 12/15 pt Dante MT Std
Typeset by Jouve (UK), Milton Keynes
Printed in Great Britain by Clays Ltd, St Ives plc

ISBN: 978-0-241-33948-0

www.greenpenguin.co.uk

MIX
Paper from
responsible sources
FSC® C018179
www.fsc.org

Penguin Random House is committed to a
sustainable future for our business, our readers
and our planet. This book is made from Forest
Stewardship Council® certified paper.

Contents

Madame du Deffand and the Idiots

Madame du Deffand's life was clearly far too long for someone who considered that her greatest misfortune was to have been born at all. It would be wrong, however, to conclude that she spent her nearly eighty-four years waiting for death. She set out the problem clearly on more than one occasion. 'To live without loving life does not make one desire its end, and it barely diminishes one's fear of losing it.' She never despaired, as did her friend and enemy Julie de Lespinasse, and she probably never suffered deep wounds of any kind. It was simply that she was bored.

While it is true that the French word *ennui* cannot be translated entirely accurately as *boredom*, it comes close enough in meaning and, of course, includes it. Madame du Deffand was bored and she fought against her boredom, which only bored her still more. Not that she gave in to it, indeed she owes her place in the history of literature to one of the weapons she used in this fierce but tedious battle: she was an indefatigable writer of letters and, it turns out, one of the finest. Her correspondence with Voltaire and with others is vast; indeed, the correspondence she maintained with the English dandy, politician and man of letters Horace Walpole comprises eight hundred and forty letters written in her hand, and these are only the ones that have come down to us. It is even more amazing when one realizes that all the letters were not, in fact, written in her hand, but dictated, for Madame du Deffand was already blind by the time she knew Walpole. Thus she never saw the man who was the object of her almost only (albeit epistolary) love, a middle-aged man, twenty-one years younger than her, and she was sixty-nine when that cross-Channel exchange of letters began. It is possible that, had she seen him, her enthusiasm and her eager wait for the postman would have been diminished, since, to judge by the portraits of him painted by Reynolds and others, the author of *The Castle of Otranto* had eyes like two hard-boiled eggs, and a nose that was too long and too far from his mouth, which was, in turn, somewhat twisted. What captivated people apparently, apart from his pleasant personality, was his voice, with the added attraction that he spoke French with a slight English accent, which made his frivolous spirit still more agreeable. Whatever the truth of the matter, the Marquise du Deffand, who, in both youth and maturity, had known no weak passions, only overwhelming ones, came to depend on letters and on herself for her survival, for, as everyone knows, the pleasure of receiving letters lies not so much in reading them as in the opportunity they bring to respond.

Madame du Deffand had been of a highly sceptical bent since childhood. Whilst at convent school, she preached irreligion to her classmates, and the

3

abbess sent for the then famous and very pious Bishop Massillon to convert her. When he emerged from their conversation, this saviour of souls said only: 'She's delightful.' When pressed by the abbess, who wanted to know what holy books they could give the girl to read, the bishop threw in the towel: 'A cheap catechism' was his glum response. At the end of her life, the Marquise tried being slightly devout, to see if this might distract her as it did other ladies of her age. Being less frivolous by nature, she did not go as far as the Maréchale de Luxembourg, who, it is said, after one glance at the Bible, exclaimed: 'The tone is absolutely frightful! What a pity the Holy Spirit had such poor taste!' Nevertheless, the Marquise had her maid read St Paul's Epistles out loud to her and grew very impatient with the apostle's style, which she judged to be inconsistent. She shouted at her maid, as if the maid were to blame: 'Can *you* make head or tail of it?' The manner in which she received her father confessor during her final illness was not exactly resigned either. She did, it is true, allow him into her house, but with these words: 'Father, you must be very pleased with me; but I ask of you just three things: no questions, no reasons, no sermons.'

During her youth, having already been married and almost immediately separated ('Feeling no love at all for one's husband is a fairly widespread misfortune'), she had taken part in a number of orgies, to which she had doubtless been introduced by her first lover, the regent Philippe d'Orléans. Thus, Madame du Deffand began her rather brief career as a libertine at the top, and, as she herself confessed, her direct and possibly exclusive relationship with the most powerful man in France lasted two whole weeks, which, in that court, was an eternity. An exaggerated and malicious description of those gatherings has this to say: 'Around supper time, the Regent would closet himself with his lovers, sometimes girls from the opera or other women of that ilk, and ten or twelve close male friends, to whom he referred as his libertines . . . Every supper was an orgy. Unbridled licence reigned; filth and impieties were the content or condiment of every conversation, until total drunkenness left the guests unable either to speak or to listen. Those who could still walk withdrew; the others were carried out bodily.'

Madame du Deffand's bad reputation pursued her for some time, but could not outrun her talent. Once past the first flush of youth, the kind of prestige she wanted was intelligence, and with the birth of her salon was born her legend: when she was very old, foreigners and young Frenchmen with a future would go to extraordinary lengths to get invited to one of her suppers, in order to be able to tell their descendants that they had met the friend of Voltaire, Montesquieu, D'Alembert, Burke, Hume and Gibbon and even of the lately deceased Fontenelle. One of those young men was Talleyrand, who, at eighteen, had a rather ingenuous view of the Marquise: 'Blindness,' he said, 'confers on the gentle placidity of her face an expression bordering on beatitude.'

Her eyes did, it seems, preserve to the last their permanent beauty, but to see in that lady 'unequalled kindness', 'great beauty' or 'beatitude' was perhaps another form of blindness, since age never changed Madame du Deffand's character, for she had always been indifferent and, on occasion, cruel. She usually had her reasons for being cruel, and her indifference was a matter of self-defence: according to those who thought they knew her well (but it would have been hard for anyone to know her very well), she was so afraid of being hurt that she always got in first and

rid herself of any person likely to hurt her. Her letters reveal the restraint with which, more than once,
she reacted to the news of the death of a friend. She
ends a letter to Walpole by saying: 'I forgot one
important fact: Voltaire has died; no one knows at
what hour or on what day; some say that it was yesterday, others the day before . . . He died of an excess
of opium which he had taken to ease the pain of his
strangury, and, I would add, of an excess of glory,
which took its toll on his feeble mechanism.' This
reveals a highly suspicious excess of coldness in
recounting the death of someone who had, over a
lifetime, been her close friend and correspondent
and who had written: 'I desire resurrection only in
order to be able to fall at the feet of Madame du Deffand.' Of the accidental death of a servant called
Colman, she remarked: 'It is a loss; he had served me
for twenty-one years and was useful to me in many
ways, I regret his passing, but then death is such a
terrible thing that it cannot but be the cause of sad-
ness. In such a mood, I thought it best not to write
to you; however, today I have changed my mind . . .'
Her reaction to the death, at the age of forty-four, of
Julie de Lespinasse, was even harsher. Her only

comment was: 'She should have died fifteen years before; then I would not have lost D'Alembert.'

While Voltaire had been her friend and Colman her servant, Julie de Lespinasse was probably her illegitimate niece and doubtless one of the people she had most loved. She had brought her from the provinces to live with her in Paris, she had introduced her into her social circle, and, in the end, Julie, a young woman as beautiful as the Marquise had once been and as intelligent as she continued to be, had formed her own salon and 'stolen' from her a few of her habitués, including the aforementioned encyclopaedist D'Alembert, for whom the Marquise had done so much when he was still unknown. D'Alembert, who tended to sarcasm, loved Julie, and that, in part, explains his defection, but not his subsequent coarseness: 'I know that the old whore Du Deffand has written to you,' he said to Voltaire, 'and she may still write to you against me and my friends, but all these old whores are good for is be laughed at and screwed.' One has the impression that D'Alembert, despite their many years of friendship, had remained untouched by the wit and expository elegance of his patroness.

Madame du Deffand loathed artificiality, although if one looks at her supposed naturalness through modern eyes, one can only think that in her circle there was, at the very least, a somewhat distorted view of what was natural. Her life followed a slightly disorderly timetable: she would get up at about five o'clock in the afternoon and, at six, receive her supper guests, of whom there might be six or seven or even twenty or thirty depending on the day; supper and talk went on until two in the morning, but since she could not bear to go to bed, she was quite capable of staying up until seven playing at dice with Charles Fox, even though she did not enjoy the game and was, at the time, seventy-three years of age. If no one else could keep her company, she would wake the coachman and have him take her for a ride along the empty boulevards. Her aversion to going to bed was due in large part to the terrible insomnia from which she had always suffered: sometimes, she would await the early morning arrival of someone who could read to her, and then, after listening to a few passages from a book, she could at last fall asleep. She always liked to be liked, but this did not mean that she could remain silent in the presence of fools:

on one famous occasion, a cardinal was expressing his amazement that, following his martyrdom, St Dionysius the Areopagite had managed to walk with his head underneath his arm all the way from Montmartre to the church that bears his name, a distance of nine kilometres that left him, the cardinal, speechless. 'But, sir,' broke in Madame du Deffand, 'the distance does not matter, it is only the first step that is difficult.' Of the ambassador from Naples she wrote: 'I miss three quarters of what he says, but since he says a great deal, the loss is bearable.' The problem was that almost everyone seemed idiotic to her, including herself: 'Yesterday, I had twelve people to supper and could only marvel at the different sorts and varieties of imbecility: we were all perfectly imbecilic, but each in our own way.' She could also be almost philanthropic: 'I find everyone loathsome.' Or even optimistic and trusting: 'One is surrounded by weapons and by enemies, and the people we call our friends are merely the ones we know would not themselves murder us, but would merely let the murderers have their way.' Or rather more general: 'All conditions and all species seem to me equally wretched, from the angel to the oyster; what is really tiresome is to have been born at all . . .' Or rather more personal: 'I am never contented with myself . . . I heartily detest myself.'

Her literary tastes were equally impatient: she adored Montaigne and Racine, and tolerated Corneille; she detested *Don Quixote* and could not read a history of Malta recommended to her by Walpole because it mentioned the Crusades, a subject that enraged her; she liked Fielding and Richardson, was passionate about *Othello* and *Macbeth*, but *Coriolanus* seemed to her 'lacking in common sense', *Julius Caesar* to be in bad taste, and *King Lear* an infernal horror that blackened the soul. Nor could she abide the young.

She continued dining in society until the end of her life, which eventually arrived on September 23, 1780, two days before her birthday. And thus, despite everything, she lived as she had wanted to live: the central moment of the day, she had said, was supper: 'one of man's four aims; I have forgotten what the other three are'.

In her last letter to Walpole, she had taken her leave of him: 'Enjoy yourself, my friend, as much as you can; do not afflict yourself in any way over my state of health; we were, for all practical purposes, lost to each other and will now never see each other again; you will regret my passing because it pleases and contents one to know that one is loved.' One has the impression that nothing, not even her own death, would have surprised Madame du Deffand. Perhaps she was not joking when she wrote to Voltaire: 'Send me, sir, a few trifles to read, but nothing about the prophets: everything they predicted I assume to have happened already.'

Nabokov in Raptures

Vladimir Nabokov probably harboured no more obsessions or antipathies than any of his writer colleagues; it may just seem that way because he was prepared to recognize, proclaim and continually foment them. This brought him something of a reputation as a misanthrope, as was bound to happen in a country as convinced of its own rectitude and tolerance as the one he adopted during the crucial years of his literary life: in the United States, especially in New England, it is not the done thing for foreigners to hold forceful opinions, still less to express them freely. 'That disagreeable old man,' is a remark that recurs among those who knew Nabokov superficially.

Nabokov spent a number of years in that part of America, always as a teacher of literature. He taught first at Wellesley College, one of the few exclusively female universities still remaining in the world, an admirable relic. It is an idyllic place, dominated by the lovely Lake Waban and the perennial autumn of its vast, changing trees and their population of squirrels. Although there are a few male teachers, on campus you see only women, most of them very young (as graduates, they're even called 'alumnae'), the daughters of ambitious, wealthy, conservative families (the students are also called 'princesses'). There, the vain illusion persists that Nabokov must have found *some* inspiration among those quasi-adolescent multitudes in skirts (although shorts were already quite common by then too) for his most famous creation, *Lolita*; but as he himself explained

on numerous occasions, the germ of that masterpiece lay in a story from his European days, *The
Enchanter*, written in Russian. His longest period of
teaching was spent at Cornell University, which is
co-ed, but no wiser for that, and Nabokov apparently
never had a very strong vocation for teaching, that
is, he took far too much trouble and too many pains
over his lectures, which he always wrote down and
then read very slowly, with the text before him on
the lectern, and as if he were talking to himself. One
of his many obsessions was the so-called Literature
of Ideas, as well as Allegory, which is why his lectures on Joyce's *Ulysses*, Kafka's *Metamorphosis*, *Anna
Karenina* or *Jekyll and Hyde* dealt mainly with the
exact plan of the city of Dublin, the exact type of
insect into which Gregor Samsa was transformed,
the exact arrangement of a railway carriage on the
night train from Moscow to St Petersburg in 1870,
and the exact appearance of the façade and interior
of Dr Jekyll's house. According to this particular
teacher, the only way of getting any pleasure out of
reading these novels was to have a very clear idea of
such things.

Given his reputation as a misanthrope, it is odd

how often the words 'pleasure', 'bliss' and 'rapture' appear in his mouth. He admitted that he wrote for two reasons: in order to achieve pleasure, bliss and rapture and to rid himself of the book on which he was currently working. Once it was started, he said, the only way to get rid of it was to finish it. On one occasion, though, he was tempted to resort to a quicker and more irrevocable method. One day in 1950, his wife, Véra, only just managed to stop him as he was heading out into the garden to burn the first chapters of *Lolita*, beset as he was with doubts and technical difficulties. On another occasion, he blamed the saving of the manuscript on his own startled conscience, convinced, he said, that the ghost of the destroyed book would pursue him for the rest of his life. Nabokov clearly had a soft spot for the novel, for, after pouring all his energies into writing it, he still found the strength to translate it into Russian, knowing full well that it would not be read in his own country for more years than he would be alive.

One must also bear in mind that the person unable to relinquish that novel was a man accustomed to relinquishing many things: according to Nabokov, all artists live in a kind of constant state of exile, whether surreptitious or manifest, although in his case, these words can only be taken ironically. He never recovered (if I can put it like that) from the loss not so much of his country of birth as of the scenes of his childhood, and although he was sure that he would never return to Russia, he sometimes toyed with the idea of getting himself a false passport and then, disguised as an American tourist, visiting his family's old country house in Rozhestveno, now converted into a Soviet school, or their house in present-day Herzen Street in what was and is once more St Petersburg. Deep down though, like all 'manifest' exiles, he knew that he would gain nothing by going back and that it would, in fact, do him harm, since it would change his unchanging memories. Doubtless because of that loss, Nabokov never really had a house of his own, in Paris or in Berlin (the cities in which he spent his first twenty years outside of Russia), or in America either, nor, at the end, in Switzerland. He lived in this last country in the Hotel Palace in Montreux, overlooking Lake Geneva, in a series of communicating rooms, which, according to various visitors, looked as temporary as if he had just arrived. One of those visitors, his fellow writer and lepidopterist Frederic Prokosch, had a long conversation with him about butterflies, their great shared passion, and although, during the conversation, the aforementioned words – pleasure, bliss and rapture – appeared more than once, the voice of his host Nabokov sounded to him 'very weary, disenchanted, and melancholy'. In the gloom of the living room, he saw him smile several times, 'perhaps with amusement or maybe in pain'.

All these perceptions must have been very subtle, since Nabokov never openly complained about his condition. Indeed, during his American years and afterwards (for he kept that nationality), he never ceased proclaiming how happy he was in the United States and how much he approved of everything in his new country. Such insistence was suspicious: on one occasion, he even made the highly improbable statement that he was 'as American as April in Arizona', and in his rooms in the Hotel Palace, the stars and stripes were flamboyantly displayed above a mantelpiece. He was conscious, too, that exiles 'end by despising the land of their exile', and he would recall how Lenin and Nietzsche, consumed by a sense of invincible nostalgia for the places of their childhood, both loathed the same country, Switzerland, that had now taken him in too.

Nevertheless – as he recounted in his extraordinary autobiography, *Speak, Memory* – when he left Russia at the age of twenty, the most painful thing was the knowledge that for weeks, possibly months, letters from his girlfriend Tamara would continue to arrive at his abandoned address in southern Crimea, where he had settled briefly before his final departure and after fleeing St Petersburg. Letters never read or answered, and that would remain so for all eternity: envelopes sealed for ever at the moment when the beloved's lips had touched them.

Before Paris and Berlin, which were packed with Russian emigrés during the 1920s and 1930s, Nabokov and his brother Sergei spent three years at Cambridge University, from which they both graduated. Nabokov's memories of that place are not exactly flattering, since what predominates is the contrast between the Russian abundance he had left behind and the deliberate meanness of things English. His fondest memories are of soccer, a sport he had always liked and which he played with considerable success not just in Russia but in Cambridge too, as goalkeeper. Apparently he saved what looked like certain goals, and was the perfect embodiment of the strange, mysterious figure of the truly legendary goalie. In his own words, he was seen as 'a fabulous, exotic being in an English footballer's disguise, composing verse in a tongue nobody understood about a remote country nobody knew'.

Nabokov must have been very reserved in his relationships with his family, as if, even in Russia, before the diaspora and before exile, he had been incapable of having much to do with his two brothers and his two sisters (perhaps rather more with his parents). He had barely any childhood memories of Sergei, who, only eleven months younger, was the nearest in age to him, and he recounted with excessive sobriety his brother's death in 1945 in Hamburg, in the Nazi concentration camp he had been taken to, accused of being a British spy, and where he died of starvation. He spoke with rather more feeling of his father who was murdered by two fascists as he was leaving a public lecture in Berlin, in 1922: the assassins' aim had been to kill the lecturer, but Nabokov's father stepped in, knocked one of them down and was felled by the other attacker's bullets.

Although Nabokov did not achieve world fame until he was fifty-six, with the absurdly scandalous publication of *Lolita*, he was always sure of his own talent. Excusing himself for being so tongue-tied, he had this to say: 'I think like a genius, I write like a distinguished author, and I speak like a child.' It bothered him enormously when people spoke of his 'influences', be it Joyce, Kafka or Proust, but especially Dostoyevsky, whom he loathed, considering him 'a cheap sensationalist, clumsy and vulgar'. In fact, he hated nearly all writers: Mann and Faulkner, Conrad and Lorca, Lawrence and Pound, Camus and Sartre, Balzac and Forster. He could just about bear Henry James, Conan Doyle, and H.G. Wells. Of Joyce's work, he admired *Ulysses*, but described *Finnegans Wake* as 'regional literature', which, generally speaking, he also abominated. He made an exception for *Petersburg* by his compatriot Biely, the first half of *A la recherche du temps perdu*, Pushkin and Shakespeare, but little else. He did not understand *Don Quixote*, and yet despite his doubts, did, in the end, find it moving. Above all, though, he hated four doctors – 'Dr Freud, Dr Zhivago, Dr Schweitzer, and Dr Castro' – especially the first, one of his bêtes noires, to whom he used to refer as 'the Viennese quack' and whose theories he considered medieval and on a par with astrology and palmistry. His obsessions and antipathies, however, went much further: he hated jazz, bullfighting, primitive masks, canned music, swimming pools, trucks, transistor radios, bidets, insecticides, yachts, the circus, hooligans, nightclubs and the roar of motorbikes, to name but a few.

He was undeniably immodest, but his arrogance seemed so genuine that it was occasionally justified and always mocking. He prided himself on being able to trace his family back to the fourteenth century, to Nabok Murza, the Russianized Tartar prince and supposed descendant of Genghis Khan. He was even prouder of his obscure literary antecedents, not so much the real (his father wrote several books) as the legendary: for example, one of his forebears had had some kind of relationship with Kleist, another with Dante, another with Pushkin, and yet another with Boccaccio. These four relationships seem altogether too much of a coincidence.

He suffered from insomnia even as a child, he was a womanizer in his youth and extremely faithful in his mature years (almost all his books are dedicated to his wife, Véra), but one should perhaps see him overall as a loner. The greatest pleasure, the greatest bliss, the greatest moments of rapture were all experienced alone: hunting butterflies, concocting chess problems, translating Pushkin, writing his books. He died on July 2, 1977 in Montreux, at the age of seventy-eight, and I learned about his death in Calle Sierpes in Seville, when I opened the newspaper as I was having breakfast in the Laredo.

He got annoyed with people who praised art that was 'sincere and simple', or who believed that the quality of art depended on its simplicity and sincerity. For him, everything was artifice, including the most authentic and deeply felt emotions, to which he himself was not immune. He put it another way too: 'In high art and pure science, detail is everything.' He never went back to Russia nor did he ever hear from Tamara. Or perhaps he did so only in the long letters he wrote to his past while ridding himself of each of his moving and artificial books.

Djuna Barnes in Silence

The very long life of Djuna Barnes was not particularly productive, at least in terms of her literature, even though, apart from a period in her youth when she worked as a journalist, it was the activity to which she devoted most of her time – well, that and maintaining prolonged silences. Her silences were both written and verbal. In the Paris of the expatriates, the

Paris of between the wars, that of Joyce and Pound and Hemingway and Fitzgerald and another eight hundred thousand would-be bohemians (mainly Americans), there are some who remember her as a constant silent presence at various crowded gatherings, looking around her with an air of shy superiority. Others, though, remember her as one of the most brilliant women of her day, guaranteed to enliven any evening, with a penchant for spot-on imitations of the famous, for impertinent remarks and laughter (a loud, strange, flamboyant laugh, which did not, it seems, last very long: it simply stopped short), for making elegant put-downs and getting tipsy.

Judging by photos taken at the time, she was not so much pretty as elegant, and this, along with her great height, made her an imposing figure, not in the ordinary sense of being very striking, but in the sense that she provoked respect. She had many affairs with men and women, although there were an even greater number of men and women whose approaches failed for the most varied of reasons, even merely literary ones. The then celebrated critic Edmund Wilson, whom she initially admired, invited her to supper one night in 1921, when she was twenty-nine. Afterwards, he suggested that she should come and live with him and that they should set off at once for Italy as the first and most acceptable step in an intellectual romance. Djuna Barnes may still have been considering this proposal when Wilson began discoursing with wild enthusiasm about the novelist Edith Wharton. And that was his great mistake, because Barnes could not abide Wharton. She may not have dismissed him entirely as a critic, but certainly as a potential lover.

On other occasions, things were less civilized: we know of a hotel porter in Rue Saint-Sulpice who tried to rape her in her room, and of a drunken journalist who picked a fight with her and her lover Thelma Wood in a café. Someone tried to drag him away; Djuna Barnes, however, had had enough: she followed the journalist out into the street, gave him a piece of her mind and received in return a blow on the chin that floored her. Undaunted, she contributed in no small measure to the drunk being overpowered and soundly beaten. A few months later, the more malicious of the gossip columns reported on how, during an argument, she had saved her male companion 'from the tougher waiters'.

Even in her more mature years she was not free from being besieged, although, by then, her most insistent suitors were women. Two writers younger than her, the now famous Anaïs Nin and Carson McCullers, submitted her – when they were not yet famous – to a real campaign of harassment, one from a distance and one from close to. Nin did so from afar and through literature, by repeatedly including a character called 'Djuna' in her work, which irritated and distressed the real Djuna, while McCullers mounted guard for a time outside her apartment. Legend has it that this then unknown young woman would spend hours moaning and sobbing at her front door, begging to be let in. Barnes, however, was unyielding and knew how to preserve her solitude. Despite Nin's clumsy tributes (she had said of Djuna: 'She sees too much, she knows too much, it is intolerable'), Barnes considered her 'a little girl lost and a sticky writer' and never deigned to receive her. As for Carson McCullers, whose work she could not possibly have known, she rewarded her with the most impenetrable of silences, apart from one evening when she presumably lost patience with the lonely hunter's constant ringing on the doorbell and said:

'Whoever is ringing this bell, please go the hell away.' The words had a temporary and, who knows, long-term effect, for poor McCullers died years later, though still somewhat prematurely, at the age of fifty.

Although Djuna Barnes's childhood and adolescence were strange and confused or confused because they were strange, and we do not know much about them, it may be that she was accustomed from a very young age to strange situations and to being besieged, especially if what people think they half-know is true, which is that at the age of seventeen or eighteen she was 'given' by her father and her grandmother (as sometimes happens in the Bible with the daughters of the patriarchs) to a man of fifty-two called Percy Faulkner, the brother of her father's mistress. This man Faulkner took her to Bridgeport for a brief period, and his surname may, who knows, have had something to do with Djuna's scant admiration for the novelist William, whom she thought sentimental. It is also true that Faulkner (the novelist) did not admire her much either, at least not officially, since in two of his books he speaks rather reproachfully of her. Many critics, however, have pointed out that Faulkner's prose style owes not a little to Barnes's own.

Other contemporaries, though, praised her openly, from T.S. Eliot, who wrote the introduction to her masterpiece, *Nightwood*, and was her champion in England, to Dylan Thomas, James Joyce (who never praised anything) and Lawrence Durrell. The latter's wild enthusiasm (he went so far as to say: 'One is glad to be living in the same epoch as Djuna Barnes') was not enough to save him from being accused of plagiarism by the writer, who detected in a text by Durrell a scene very like one she herself had written. It was probably true, but it was doubtless more an homage than an act of plagiarism. This happened in the 1960s, and she apparently saw such thefts everywhere. Shortly before, in the 1950s, she received Malcolm Lowry in her apartment and he described the visit in a letter. Even though he himself was a complete mess, she seemed to him even more lost: he found her painting some sort of semi-female male demon on the wall; she told him off for the success of *Under the Volcano*, gave him six bottles of beer to drink one after the other, and confessed her fears about her own novel *Nightwood*, which she had published sixteen years earlier, but since when, she said, she had written nothing else. Although he had mixed feelings about the book (a technical masterpiece, but also somehow monstrous), Lowry admitted that, all in all, 'her or him or It' was an admirable, if terrifying, tragic being, 'possessing both integrity and honour'. Lowry clearly left the apartment feeling somewhat confused, or perhaps it was the fault of those generous beers.

It is hardly surprising that Djuna Barnes should have considered her first name as so unequivocally hers when Anaïs Nin took the liberty of using it, for most of the names in her family seem to have been chosen precisely so that no one else could usurp them. Suffice it to say that among her own siblings and ancestors were the following extravagant examples, which, in many cases, do not even give a clue as to the gender of the person bearing them: Urlan, Niar, Unade, Reon, Hinda, Zadel, Gaybert, Culmer, Kilmeny, Thurn, Zendon, Saxon, Shangar, Wald and Llewellyn. At least the last name is recognized in Wales. Perhaps it is understandable that, on reaching adulthood, some members of the Barnes family adopted banal nicknames like Bud or Charlie. It's possible that the names owe their origin to some mystery, given that there was a vague tradition of eccentric spiritualism in the family. One of Djuna's grandfathers even had acolytes, only a few, but one of whom was the great Houdini.

Djuna Barnes had no children and was married only once, to a fellow called Courtenay Lemon, a marriage that lasted about three years, but only just. Apparently he was an easy-going sort with a slight tendency to be overweight. He drank a lot of gin, was a socialist, wrote dull, cliché-ridden pamphlets and aspired to formulating 'a philosophy of criticism' which he never finished. Djuna Barnes had more male lovers than female, but if she had one great love – which is doubtful – it was the sculptress Thelma Wood. They lived together in Paris for a number of years and always attracted attention when they walked along the boulevards: two foreign women, elegant, determined, disdainful, Thelma Wood with her enormous feet which no one, meeting her for the first time, ever failed to notice, especially those who danced with her and had to keep a careful eye on them. Wood was even more cutting than Barnes, and more boastful too:

when the Canadian writer John Glassco brazenly admired her body while they were dancing (those giant feet) and asked her bluntly to come to bed with him, adding, 'Sorry, I hope I'm not frightening you,' she replied: 'Frighten me? No one frightens Thelma Wood.' Perhaps she was one of those strange people who talk about themselves in the third person. Thelma was a drunk and a spendthrift, and, worse still, was in the habit of losing, even before she could spend it, the money she took from Djuna, who, on many nights, had to go out into the streets looking for Thelma, feeling as jealous as she was worried, until she found her at last in some tricky situation and took her back home exhausted.

Among the men, it is worth highlighting her love affair with Putzi Hanfstaengl, a German who had studied at Harvard and who, twenty years later, became the official jester at the court of Adolf Hitler. Even though Djuna loathed him (Hitler, that is, not Putzi), they remained in touch, and Barnes thus became the first person among the allies to know about the lower abdominal shortcomings of the otherwise immeasurable Führer. A photo survives from 1928 which shows them together (Djuna and Putzi, not Adolf): he is wearing a bowtie, has a large nose and is very cross-eyed; the fact is he looks like a murderer.

Djuna Barnes's life lasted ninety years and for far too many of them she either did not want or could not have any lovers and so she had no alternative but to remain silent. Her apartment in New York was her inaccessible refuge. There she received letters and the cheques with which her friend, the multimillionairess Peggy Guggenheim, kept her provided for years, as well as the occasional call from publishers wanting to reprint her few books and with whom she invariably grew indignant. (She got indignant with Henry Miller too, whom she thought was a swine.) Sometimes she would work three or four eight-hour days just to produce two or three lines of verse, and the slightest noise would ruin her concentration for the rest of the day and plunge her into despair. According to one of her biographers, she spent more than fifteen thousand days, that is, more than forty years, in her apartment in Patchin Place. And we know that most of them, days and years, passed in total silence without her exchanging a single word with anyone. Just the noise of the typewriter and those lines still unread. In 1931, long before those forty years began, she had written: 'I like my human experience served up with a little silence and restraint. Silence makes experience go further, and, when it does die, gives it that dignity common to a thing one had touched and not vanished.'

No one saw very much of her during this interminable old age. She was afraid of the adolescents who hung around in the streets. She had such a horror of beards that she even phoned a future visitor and demanded that he shave his off (she had enquired about his appearance) before he came to see her. She considered age to be an exercise in interpretation, but she also thought that the old ought to be killed off. 'There should be a law,' she said. The law had its way in that apartment on the night of June 18, 1982, six days after its tenant had become a nonagenarian. The few people who visited her before that date spent long hours with her and always ended up with a headache. 'I've been told that I give everyone I talk to a headache,' she said. The response of the afflicted visitor was: 'You're so intense!' And she said: 'Yes, I know.'

Oscar Wilde After Prison

According to all who met him, the hand that Oscar Wilde proffered by way of greeting was as soft as a cushion, or, rather, as flabby as old plasticine and somewhat greasy, and left one with a sense of having been sullied by shaking it. Others have said that his skin was grubby and bilious and that, when he spoke, he had the unfortunate habit of pinching and

tugging at his rather ample double chin. Many
people, whether prejudiced or not, found him, at
first sight, repellent, but all agree that this feeling
vanished as soon as Wilde began to speak, and was
replaced by another feeling entirely, one of vague
maternalism or open admiration, of unconditional
sympathy. Even the Marquess of Queensberry – who
would, in the end, cause Wilde to go to prison and
to cease writing altogether – succumbed to his personal charm when he encountered him at the Café
Royal, where Wilde was lunching with the Marquess's son, Lord Alfred Douglas, the Marquess
having gone there with the intention of removing
the latter from Wilde's pernicious influence. As
recounted by Douglas himself – known to his friends
as 'Bosie' – Queensberry was in the worst possible
mood when he arrived, seething with hatred and
contempt for Wilde, but within ten minutes 'he was
eating out of his hand' and the following day he
sent a note to his son 'Bosie' withdrawing everything
he had ever said or written about his friend: 'I don't
wonder you are so fond of him,' he said, 'he is a
wonderful man.'

It is true, however, that this second impression did

not last very long, and before both gentlemen took each other to court – culminating in Wilde's infamous and unhappy defeat – they had at least one other, far more tense encounter. On this occasion, the Marquess, who has passed into history for setting down the rules for that 'sport of gentlemen', boxing, and for having – possibly – deprived the English public of some of its favourite comedies, turned up at Wilde's house accompanied by a boxer, who was not only a professional, but a champion to boot. The Marquess himself had been a good amateur lightweight, and was still known at the time as a spirited horseman and mad-keen hunter. In opposition to this rude pair stood Wilde and his diminutive servant, a seventeen-year-old lad who looked like a miniature. There was no need, however, to come to blows. Once the 'screaming scarlet Marquess', as Wilde called him, had said what he had to say regarding his mission to rescue his corrupted son, Wilde rang the bell for his tiny, child major-domo and told him: 'This is the Marquess of Queensberry, the most infamous brute in London. You are never to allow him to enter my house again,' after which he opened the door and ordered the two men to leave. The Marquess obeyed, and it did not even occur to the boxer, who appears to have been both good-hearted and respectful, to intervene in a discussion between gentlemen.

Oscar Wilde was, then, a strong man, despite his apparent softness, which began, according to legend, in his most tender years, when his mother, the Irish activist and poetess Lady Wilde, disappointed at having giving birth to a second son instead of the little girl she had wanted and unable easily to resign herself to this fact, continued to dress Oscar in girlish clothes for far longer than was perhaps advisable. There is another legend about his strength and physical power according to which, when he was a student in Oxford, he received in his rooms the unwanted visit of four louts from Magdalen College who had come from a drunken party and were out to have fun at his expense. To the surprise of the more timorous members of the group, who had stayed behind at the foot of the stairs as spectators, their four burly friends, who had gone up with the intention of destroying the aesthetic garb and Chinese porcelain of that affected son of Ireland, all came tumbling back down the stairs, one after the other.

It seems that many people have lied about Wilde

in their time, and one can only put this down to the many contradictions in the information that we have about him. However, maybe the following anecdote told by Ford Madox Ford does not necessarily contradict his reputation for boldness: after leaving prison, and during his final years in Paris, Wilde was frequently the butt of student jibes when he walked through Montmartre. An *apache* called Bibi La Touche, accompanied by some other thugs, used to come over to him and tell him that he had taken a fancy to Wilde's ebony walking stick, with its ivory inlays and its handle in the shape of an elephant, and that, if Wilde did not surrender it immediately, he would be murdered on his way home. According to Ford, Wilde would then weep, the tears pouring down his great cheeks, and invariably surrender his stick. The following morning, the *apaches* would return it to his hotel, only to demand it again a few days later. Maybe all the legends are true, bearing in mind how much Wilde, the ex-convict, had changed. Perhaps he had learned to be afraid in prison, and he was, at any rate, a man prematurely aged, with only what money his most faithful friends could find for him, too lazy to work (that is, to write), exasperatingly querulous and faintly comic. During this period, he adopted the name Sebastian Melmoth, published only his famous *Ballad of Reading Gaol*, grew ever deafer, had coarse, reddened skin and walked as if his feet hurt him, leaning always on that much-stolen stick. His clothes were not as resplendent as they had been in the past, and he had succumbed at last to the obesity that had stalked him for so long; i n a photo taken of him standing in front of St Peter's in Rome, three years before his death, his whole figure is dominated and made ludicrous by a minuscule hat that cruelly emphasizes his very large head, the head which, in his youth, had been crowned by long, artistic locks and capacious plumed hats.

The only thing he did not lose was his gift for conversation, and they say that he presided over gatherings and suppers with the same firm hand and rich variety of anecdote as he had during his years of greatest glory in London, the years when he was a playwright. It was not just that he came out with endless witticisms, invented improbable puns, and improvised maxims each more brilliant than the last, it seems that he was also an extraordinary teller of tales, far better than he ever was as a writer. At any social event, he was the one who talked, the only one, and yet, whenever he was alone with someone, that person always had the feeling that he had never been listened to with more attention, interest and pity, if pity was what was required. It is true that, as regards his wordplay, he was often accused of plagiarism: Pater, it was claimed, or Whistler or Shaw, had said the same thing before him. This was doubtless true in many instances (he certainly imitated Whistler, whom he at first revered and with whom he later fell out), but the fact is that his ingenious comments, whoever they may originally have belonged to, only became famous when spoken by him.

Wilde's bisexuality is a proven fact, although the scandal of his trials tends to make one think of him as the pure apostle and modern proto-martyr of homosexuality. However, not only did he marry Constance Lloyd, with whom he had two children, there has been much talk of the syphilis he caught from a female prostitute in his youth and of an early disappointment with a young Irishwoman whom he courted doggedly for two years, at the end of which time she married Bram Stoker. (One can only conclude, incidentally, that the young woman in question had a taste for strong emotions, and, having hesitated between the future authors of *The Picture of Dorian Gray* and *Dracula*, she opted, in the end, for immortal vampirism rather than a pictorial and not very enduring pact with the Devil.) And several of his friends and acquaintances were amazed when the scandal broke and they learned what the charges were: they would never have suspected him of such proclivities, they said, despite Wilde's repeated professions of Hellenism from his student days on and ever since his trip to Greece, which resulted in a photograph of the traveller in full-skirted local dress and in his formal embrace of paganism, to the detriment of the Catholicism he had been considering taking up shortly before. He had even adorned his rooms at Oxford with pictures of the Pope and of Cardinal Manning, but when he actually visited the former, at an audience in Rome arranged by his extremely Catholic and extremely wealthy friend Hunter Blair, he maintained a sullen silence throughout and thought the whole encounter dreadful; afterwards, he closeted himself in his hotel room and emerged bearing an apposite sonnet. The worst came later: as they were passing the Protestant cemetery, Wilde insisted on stopping and prostrating himself before the grave of Keats, a far humbler obeisance than he had offered to the very pious Pius IX.

Little is known of Constance Lloyd Wilde, except that she viewed her husband with a mixture of disapproval and sweetness. On the other hand, a great deal is known about Lord Alfred Douglas, or 'Bosie', thanks largely to the various books he himself wrote during his long life (he died in 1945 at the age of seventy-five), divided equally between poetry and volumes of more or less autobiographical and justificatory prose. As a young man he was long on ringlets and short on intelligence, and, in later years, he lost the ringlets, but gained not a jot in intelligence: he became a Catholic and a puritan, and his judgement about what happened seems confused to say the least. It was his fate to live for far too long marked by a scandal in which he was only the reluctant co-protagonist, but he never did anything to justify his taking centre stage for any other reason. Two years after Wilde's death, he married a poetess, and so one might say that he made an odd marriage – of versifiers. His bête noire was Robert Ross, who not only manipulated and kept the long letter that Wilde had written to 'Bosie' from prison and which is now known as *De Profundis*, but was the remote instigator of that whole tragedy, having initiated the youthful Wilde into sex in its most Hellenistic vein.

Wilde's witticisms are legion, and most have found too warm a reception in quotation heaven to repeat them here. Indeed, even now, he is attributed with ingenious comments that never even occurred to him. This description of a hard day in a writer's life is, however, definitely his: 'This morning,' he said, 'I took out a comma, and this afternoon, I put it back again.'

Later, he seemed to take these words literally, after leaving the prison in which he had spent two years doing hard labour. Although it was clear that if he wrote a new comedy or a novel, money would rain down on him and his poverty would be at an end, he had neither the strength nor the will to write. As he put it, he had known suffering and could not sing its praises; he hated it, but he had known it, and that is why he could not now sing the praises of what had always hitherto inspired him: pleasure and joy. 'Everything that happens to me,' he said, 'is symbolic and irrevocable.' During those years, André Gide described him as 'a poisoned creature'. He drank too much, which further irritated the reddened skin of his face and body: he often had to scratch himself, for which he apologized. He wrote to a friend: 'I am more like a great ape than ever, I hope you will give me a lunch and not a nut.'

Six years before his fall from grace, he had written this: 'Life sells everything too dear, and we buy the most wretched of its secrets at a monstrous, infinite price.' He stopped paying that price on November 30, 1900, when he died in Paris at the age of forty-six, after a death agony that lasted more than two months. The cause of his death was an ear infection which later spread and was vaguely syphilitic in origin. Legend has it that shortly before he died, he called for champagne and, when it was brought in to him, said cheerfully: 'I am dying beyond my means.' He lies in the Paris cemetery of Père Lachaise, and on his grave, presided over by a sphinx, there is never any shortage of the flowers due to all martyrs.

Emily Brontë, the Silent Major

The life of Emily Brontë was so short and silent and is now so remote that very little is known about her, not that this has stopped her biographer compatriots from retelling her life in fat and usually rather vacuous volumes. Although there are, as far as history is concerned, always three Brontë sisters, there were, in fact, five, to whom, as people all too frequently forget, one should also add their brother Branwell, who, however disastrous and alcoholic he may have been, was nonetheless important in the life of the most famous of the sisters. The two sisters no one ever mentions were called Maria and Elizabeth, and they died from tuberculosis, one after the other, when they were still children. In a rather Dickensian episode, they were harshly treated by their teachers shortly before they died, being punished and insulted and forced to get out of bed when they were already ill. Posterity has laid a strange reproach at Emily's door: namely, that, despite being the school favourite, she failed to intercede for the victims, and remained silent before this rank injustice. The reproach is particularly unfair given that the author of *Wuthering Heights* was not yet six years old, five and four years younger, respectively, than her two ill-treated sisters. After them came Charlotte and then Branwell, and after Emily, Anne, the youngest, the three surviving sisters all becoming novelists, while Branwell became merely a frustrated poet. Their mother had died when Emily was three years old, and they were all brought up by their Irish-born father, who, as a writer of sermons, was not unconnected with literature himself. Other less pious members of the family initiated the sisters into the oral tradition, with the Irish storytellers' habitual preference for tales of ghosts and demons and goblins. This was doubtless Emily's first contact with the supernatural, which hovers over her one novel from first page to last.

Her silence apparently caused her more than one upset and gave her a reputation for arrogance: from adolescence on, Emily would often answer only in monosyllables or not at all, which caused some people to shun her and drew protests from her sisters. She was, however, her father's favourite, as demonstrated by the fact that he taught her how to fire a pistol and often took her out target shooting (to which she became addicted). Mr Brontë – who exoticized his original name of Brunty when he was studying (where else?) at Oxford (perhaps because *bronte* means 'thunder' in Greek) – was thought to be eccentric and austere and, although these extant reports come from rather unreliable sources (that is, sources with an axe to grind), it is said that, in his zeal, he refused to give his daughters meat to eat and condemned them to a diet of potatoes; they say that one rainy night, after he had discovered that the girls were wearing dainty boots given to them by a friend, he burned the boots because he deemed them too luxurious; he tore to shreds a silk dress that his wife kept in a trunk, more to look at than to wear; and, on one occasion, he sawed the backs off various chairs to make them into stools. If all this is true, then the Brontë sisters did very well in not turning to drink like their brother. And regardless of whether or not it is true, one thing is clear, Mr Brontë was also extremely affectionate towards them and, indeed, took the trouble to educate them: he would have them put on masks and would then interrogate them, believing that, with their faces covered, they would become used to responding freely and boldly. He once asked Emily what he should do with Branwell when he was at his most impossible: 'Reason with him, and when he won't listen to reason, whip him.' She was six years old at the time, and clearly had a proclivity for drastic measures. When she was older, she punched her dog Keeper in the face and eyes – they swelled right up – to stop the dog from going for her throat after she had reprimanded him. On another occasion, she separated the same dog and a stray, with whom it had become embroiled in a fight, by sprinkling pepper on their snouts, which indicates that, despite her silence, she was a very decisive woman. It was no coincidence that her sisters nicknamed her 'The Major'. Nevertheless, and despite being the tallest in the family, she was sometimes described as rather a fragile creature with precarious health. After a stay of eight months with her sisters in Belgium, there were also some fears for her mental health, but that is a fairly commonplace accusation in family disputes. She loved Walter Scott and was a devotee of both Shelley and the night, which is why she slept very little, in order to enjoy it to the full.

It was her sister Charlotte who, not without great difficulty, managed to persuade her to publish her poems. Later on, all three sisters, under the pseudonyms Currer, Ellis and Acton Bell, sent their respective first novels to the publishers. The only one that was not, initially, accepted was Charlotte's, but her second novel, *Jane Eyre*, was. The reviews of *Wuthering Heights* were very positive, but no one dared hail it as the masterpiece that time has shown it to be.

In 1848, a year after its publication, Emily often had to go to the Black Bull Inn to fetch Branwell and help him back home. Her concern was merely routine, and neither she, through lack of foresight, nor Charlotte, out of a spirit of revenge, did anything serious about curing Branwell, who went to his grave not long afterwards, having spent periods racked by horrific coughing fits and terrible insomnia. Emily followed him only three months later, and although a housemaid declared that 'Miss Emily died of a broken heart for love of her brother', giving rise to speculations about incest, it is more likely that Emily Brontë knew nothing in life of the passions she so skilfully described in her semi-incestuous *Wuthering Heights*.

During her illness, she refused to have any treatment or to be seen by a doctor and once again plunged into long silences, prepared to let nature take its course, although nature proved far from benign. On December 19, she insisted on leaving her bed and getting dressed, then she sat down by the fire in her room and started combing her long, abundant tresses. Her comb fell into the flames, and since she did not have the strength to pick it up, the bedroom was filled with the smell of burning bone. Afterwards, she went down to the living room and there, sitting on the sofa, she died at two o'clock in the afternoon, having refused to go back to bed. She was only thirty years old and she wrote nothing more.